jams AND preserves

jams AND preserves

gina steer

Love Food™ is an imprint of Parragon Books Ltd

Parragon
Queen Street House
4 Queen Street
Bath BA1 1HE, UK

Copyright © Parragon Books Ltd 2007

Love Food™ and the accompanying heart device is a trademark of Parragon Books Ltd.

ISBN: 978-1-4054-9246-1
Printed in China

Produced by the Bridgewater Book Company Ltd

Photography: Clive Bozzard-Hill
Home economists: Valerie Barrett and Sandra Baddeley

Notes for the Reader
This book uses imperial, metric, and US cup measurements. Follow the same units of measurement throughout; do not mix imperial and metric. All spoon measurements are level: teaspoons are assumed to be 5 ml, and tablespoons are assumed to be 15 ml. Unless otherwise stated, milk is assumed to be whole, eggs and individual vegetables such as potatoes are medium, and pepper is freshly ground black pepper. The times given are an approximate guide only.

The author would like to thank Tate & Lyle and Ocean Spray, and her family and friends who tasted enthusiastically all the preserves in this book.

contents

Introduction   6

Jams and Conserves   12

Jellies   28

Marmalade   42

Curds and Butters   56

Chutneys, Pickles, and Relishes   68

Preserves   84

Index   96

introduction

What could be more satisfying than having a row of homemade preserves in your pantry? Whether it is a jam, chutney, pickle, relish, or conserve, there really is nothing better. Why? You may ask. Well, it is simple. Making your own preserves ensures that you have total control over the quality of the ingredients used, as well as ensuring that there are no hidden extras, such as artificial colors or flavorings. Plus, of course, if you grow your own fruit or vegetables, it is a great way to use your own produce, especially when you find you have a glut of a particular food. Preserves also make an excellent gift and one that everyone would be proud to give and more than happy to receive.

Equipment

It is not strictly necessary to buy special equipment for making preserves, but if you plan to make a few there are several pieces that make life just that little bit easier.

Large pan—The first piece you need is a very large pan, about 5–10 quarts in capacity. This needs to be heavy and made of aluminum, stainless steel, or copper. Look for a wide diameter pan, which allows for maximum evaporation when boiling to setting point, and one that has two handles on either side or a large handle that goes from one side to the other for ease of handling. A pan with a non-reactive interior, such as enamel, aluminum, stainless steel, or nonstick, is best when making chutney or pickles. This will ensure the acidic content does not react with the pan. When using the pan for jams, jellies, or conserves, you need to make sure that it is large enough. It needs to be no more than half full after the sugar has dissolved, otherwise the contents will boil over when you are boiling to setting point. The pan also needs a lid, which is useful when cooking fruits and vegetables that need a long simmering time. If you use a smaller pan, the preserve will take longer to reach setting point because the surface area is not as large.

Long-handled wooden spoon—An essential piece of equipment that enables the successful stirring of fruits or vegetables without the spoon falling into the hot liquid. Look for wooden spoons that are at least 12 inches/30 cm; better still, those that are 15 inches/38 cm.

Long-handled slotted spoon—These are ideal for skimming off any stones or scum that floats to the top when boiling to setting point.

Jam or candy thermometer—When making jams, jellies, or conserves, the hot liquid needs to be brought to setting point. Using the thermometer is more accurate than the saucer method (see page 10).

Jelly bag and stand—This is for straining off the juices from the fruits that have been simmered slowly to extract all the liquid possible. The juice is then boiled with sugar to make the jelly. You can improvise by suspending a jelly bag from the legs of an upturned chair or stool. The stand, which it is possible to buy, is attached to the sides of a large bowl. It is essential that the jelly bag is scalded with boiling water before using and the contents should be left in a draft-free place and not squeezed, to enable all the juice to drip through. This will ensure a cloud-free jelly. Wash thoroughly after use and scald each time. The bowl should also be scalded before use.

Funnel—This has a wide neck and sits comfortably in the neck of a jar, enabling the jars to be filled with minimal spillage.

Slicer—This can be either an attachment to a freestanding mixer or a tabletop slicer. Many food processors also have a slicing attachment. This is useful for making marmalade. The peel of Seville oranges is far tougher than other citrus fruits and it needs to be finely shredded to make it palatable. Some recipes soak the shredded peel for a long period or simmer for 30 minutes covered with water before using in the preserve. The peel can be cut into fine shreds with a sharp kitchen knife, but using a slicer is easier.

Cherry pitter—Useful when making preserves with fresh cherries, this will help to prevent your hands from being stained by the juice.

Strainer—If you need to use a strainer, ensure that it is nylon to avoid any tainting of the food. Metal could discolor the fruits.

Jars—Clean jars are an essential part of preserving. It is a good idea to save the jars from commercial products. Make sure the jars are scrupulously clean and sterilized before use. When required, wash well in plenty of hot soapy water and rinse thoroughly in very hot water to remove all traces of soap, then dry off. Place upturned jars on a cookie sheet in a warm oven at 275°F/140°C for 15 minutes to sterilize them, then place the sterilized jars upside down on a clean kitchen towel until required. Once setting point has been reached, let the preserve stand for 10–15 minutes before potting. Fill the jars while they are still warm. Any glass jars can be used as long as they are warm and sterilized.

Cheesecloth—This is ideal for making small bags to enclose seeds, spices, or other ingredients that need removing after boiling. Cut out a square: the size will be governed by the amount to be tied up. Place the ingredients in the center and fold up into a pouch. Tie with a long piece of string and attach to one of the pan handles and ensure that the bag is immersed in the liquid. It is then easy to remove at the end of cooking.

Covers—Once made, the preserves should be covered immediately with a wax disk and left until cold. Once completely cold, cover with cellophane covers that are lightly dampened, then secure with an elastic band. Alternatively, use tight-fitting, screw-top lids. Don't use metallic lids when making pickles and chutneys. Label and date clearly, then store in cool, dark cupboards or the pantry.

Testing for a set

The easiest way to test is with a jam or candy thermometer, where the preserve needs to reach 220°F/105°C. Place the thermometer in the pan when boiling rapidly, until the mercury reaches the correct temperature. Alternatively, try the saucer test. Place a few saucers in the refrigerator when the preserve starts to boil. Then, when it has been boiling rapidly for the stated time, place a small teaspoonful of the mixture on a cold saucer and let stand for a couple of minutes. Take the pan off the heat when testing for a set. If the jam on the saucer wrinkles when a clean finger is pushed across the surface of it, then setting point has been reached. If it is not ready, return to a rolling boil and retest in a few minutes. Take care not to overboil.

Ingredients

The condition of the produce used is extremely important when making preserves. The fruit needs to be ripe but still firm, without any rotten or bad pieces. Vegetables also need to be free from bruises or damaged pieces. Both fruit and vegetables need to be very fresh, but it is possible to freeze them for later use. This is very useful when making marmalade; Seville oranges (sour oranges) are seasonal and appear in the stores only around the end of January. Buy and freeze immediately, then thaw and use within 6 months. When using for marmalade, use a little extra than the recipe to allow for any loss of pectin while frozen.

Setting agents—Jams, jellies, marmalades, and conserves will set only if they have the correct amount of setting agent and sugar. The setting agent is pectin—either natural or commercial. Commercial pectin is made from apples and is in liquid form. It is generally added after boiling and is normally used for fruits that have a low natural pectin level. It is also used for preserves where the fruit is only lightly boiled so as to retain larger pieces of fruit. Fruits with a high pectin content include black currants, cooking apples, crab apples, cranberries, damsons, gooseberries, lemons, limes, Seville oranges, quinces, and red currants. Fruits with a medium pectin content include dessert apples, apricots, blueberries, blackberries, greengages, loganberries, plums, and raspberries. Fruits with a low pectin content include bananas, carrots, cherries, figs, grapes, marrows, melons, peaches, nectarines, pineapple, rhubarb, and strawberries.

Sugar—Use either cane or beet sugar, as both work equally well. If it just says "sugar" in a recipe, use granulated sugar. Often this will mean that the recipe will be using pectin as well.

Lemon and lime juice—These contain a high pectin level and can be added to the pan with the fruit to help with the set. Citric acid can also be used. It is important that the correct amount of pectin acid and sugar are used, as both are imperative to obtain a good set.

Vinegar—This is a preserving agent and is the most important part of any pickle or chutney. Use the best quality, as this will have a high acetic quality. Distilled or white vinegar is best used for preserves where a lighter color is required. Most pickles and chutneys improve with keeping for at least two weeks to let the flavors mature. Infusing with spices can also enhance both vinegars.

Salt—Table or cooking salt is used to make a brine solution to soak vegetables or some fruits that are going to be used in pickles. Ensure that the foods soaked in brine are thoroughly rinsed before use.

Jams and conserves are made from fruits and sugar boiled together to produce a delicious spread that can be used on breads, tarts, cakes, and desserts. The high content of sugar preserves the fruit and helps to prevent the growth of bacteria. This is why reduced-sugar jams should be kept in the refrigerator once opened and used quickly. Jams with a higher sugar content will keep in a cool cupboard or pantry for two to three months if the lids are screwed down tightly.

jams and conserves

Other flavors can be added, if liked, to the recipes in this chapter. Spices to try are lightly bruised lemongrass stalks, star anise, cardamom, or vanilla beans. Tie in a small piece of cheesecloth and discard after boiling.

Classic strawberry jam

MAKES about 1 lb/450 g

3 lb 5 oz/1.5 kg ripe, unblemished whole strawberries, hulled and rinsed

2 freshly squeezed lemons, juice strained

3 lb 5 oz/1.5 kg sugar

1 tsp butter

Place the strawberries in a large pan with the lemon juice, then simmer over gentle heat for 15–20 minutes, stirring occasionally, until the fruit has collapsed and is very soft.

Add the sugar and heat, stirring occasionally, until the sugar has completely dissolved. Add the butter, then bring to a boil and boil rapidly for 10–20 minutes, or until the setting point is reached.

Let cool for 8–10 minutes, then skim. Pot into warmed sterilized jars and cover the tops with wax disks. When completely cold, cover with cellophane or lids, then label and store in a cool place.

Cook's tip: Other flavors can be added if liked. Add 2 lightly bruised lemongrass stalks and 4 lightly bruised green cardamom pods. Discard the spices before potting.

Spicy blueberry jam

MAKES about 3 lb 5 oz/1.5 kg

1 lb 8 oz/675 g blueberries, rinsed

1 cup freshly squeezed orange juice

2 whole star anise

1 cinnamon stick, lightly bruised

1 lb 2 oz/500 g granulated sugar

¾ cup liquid pectin

Place the blueberries in a large pan with the orange juice. Tie the spices up in a small piece of cheesecloth and add to the pan, then simmer over gentle heat for 20 minutes, or until very soft.

Add the sugar and cook gently, stirring occasionally, until the sugar has completely dissolved. Bring to a boil and boil for 3 minutes, then remove from the heat and stir in the pectin. Let cool slightly.

Discard the spices, then pot into warmed sterilized jars and cover the tops with wax disks. When completely cold, cover with cellophane or lids, then label and store in a cool place.

Cook's tip: Try using a vanilla bean, split open, in place of the cinnamon and star anise.

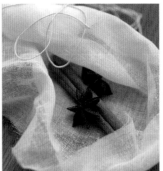

Cherry with brandy jam

Coarsely chop the cherries and place in a large pan with the lemon juice. If using citric or tartaric acid, add to the pan with the water. Place the pan over gentle heat, then cover and simmer gently for 20 minutes, or until the cherries have collapsed and are very soft.

Add the sugar and heat, stirring frequently, until the sugar has completely dissolved. Add the butter and brandy, then bring to a boil and boil rapidly for 3 minutes. Remove from the heat and stir in the pectin.

Let cool for 10 minutes, then pot into warmed sterilized jars and cover the tops with wax disks. When completely cold, cover with cellophane or lids, then label and store in a cool place.

Cook's tip: Other spirits or liqueurs can be used in place of the brandy. Try Kirsch, Cointreau, or a whisky liqueur.

MAKES about 5 lb/2.25 kg

4 lb/1.8 kg dark sour cherries, such as Morello, rinsed and pitted

1/2 cup freshly squeezed lemon juice or 1 1/2 tsp citric or tartaric acid

2/3 cup water (optional)

2 lb 12 oz/1.25 kg granulated sugar

1 tsp butter

4 tbsp brandy

1 cup liquid pectin

Plum jam

MAKES about 5 lb/2.25 kg

3 lb 5 oz/1.5 kg ripe but firm plums, rinsed

2 cups water

3 lb 5 oz/1.5 kg sugar

1 tsp butter

Discard any damaged plums, then cut in half and remove the pits. Crack a few of the pits open and remove the kernels and set aside.

Place the plums, reserved kernels, and water in a large pan. Bring to a boil, then reduce the heat and simmer for 40 minutes, or until soft and pulpy. Add the sugar and heat gently, stirring frequently, until the sugar has completely dissolved, then add the butter. Bring to a boil and boil rapidly for 10–15 minutes, or until the setting point is reached.

Let cool for 8 minutes, then pot into warmed sterilized jars and cover the tops with wax disks. When completely cold, cover with cellophane or lids, then label and store in a cool place.

Cook's tip: Add some spices to give a distinctive flavor, such as 6 lightly cracked cardamom pods or 2–3 lightly bruised lemongrass stalks.

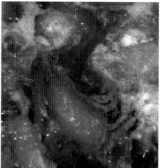

Peach and passion fruit jam

MAKES about 5 lb 8 oz/2.5 kg

2 lb/900 g ripe, firm peaches, rinsed

4 ripe passion fruits

²/₃ cup freshly squeezed lemon juice

2 lb/900 g sugar

Make a small cross at the stalk end of each peach and place in a large bowl. Cover with boiling water and let stand for 2–3 minutes. Drain and let cool. When cool enough to handle, peel off the skins. Cut the peaches in half and discard the pits. Place the fruit in a large pan. Halve the passion fruits and scoop out the pulp, then add to the peaches.

Add the lemon juice and sugar, then place over gentle heat and simmer for 30 minutes, or until the fruit is soft and pulpy. Bring to a boil and boil rapidly for 15 minutes, or until the setting point is reached.

Let cool for 10–15 minutes before potting into warmed sterilized jars and cover the tops with wax disks. When completely cold, cover with cellophane or lids, then label and store in a cool place.

Cook's tip: Passion fruit are ripe and ready to use when very wrinkled.

Quick apricot jam

Place the apricots in a microwaveable bowl and add the lemon juice and water, then cover and cook on high for 5–6 minutes, or until very soft. Remove and pour into a large pan. Alternatively, cook the apricots with the lemon juice in a heavy-bottomed pan for 20–25 minutes, or until soft.

Add the sugar and cook gently, stirring occasionally, until the sugar has completely dissolved. Stir in the cranberries and bring to a boil, then boil for 15 minutes, or until the setting point is reached. Remove from the heat and let stand for 5 minutes. Stir in the slivered almonds.

Pot into warmed sterilized jars and cover the tops with wax disks. When completely cold, cover with cellophane or lids, then label and store in a cool place.

Cook's tip: The kernels from the pits can be added if liked. Crack open a few pits, then remove the kernels and blanch before adding to the pan with the fruit.

MAKES about 6 lb/2.7 kg

4 lb/1.8 kg ripe apricots, rinsed and chopped, pits discarded

²/₃ cup freshly squeezed lemon juice

1 cup water

4 lb/1.8 kg sugar

¹/₃ cup dried cranberries

¹/₄ cup slivered almonds

Melon and ginger jam

MAKES about 2 lb/900 g

1 Galia melon, about 1 lb/450 g
(peeled weight)

1 large wedge watermelon, about
1 lb/450 g (peeled weight)

2 lb/900 g granulated sugar

⅓ cup lemon juice

3-inch/7.5-cm piece fresh
gingerroot, peeled and grated

½ cup liquid pectin

Peel the melons, discarding the seeds, and finely chop the flesh. Place in a large bowl and sprinkle with 1 lb/450 g of sugar and the lemon juice. Cover and leave overnight.

The next day, place the melon with the liquid that has been extracted overnight into a large pan, together with the grated ginger, and simmer over gentle heat for 30 minutes, or until very soft. Add the remaining sugar and heat, stirring occasionally, until the sugar has completely dissolved. Bring to a boil and boil rapidly for 3 minutes. Remove the pan from the heat and stir in the pectin.

Let cool for 10 minutes, then pot into warmed sterilized jars and cover the tops with wax disks. When completely cold, cover with cellophane or lids, then label and store in a cool place.

Cook's tip: Add some chopped preserved ginger to the pan with the pectin.

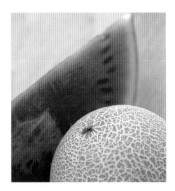

Jellies can be served with meat and vegetable dishes as well as sweet ones, and provide a delicious addition to any meal. When making jellies, the fruits do not need much preparation, as they are strained through a jelly bag to extract the juice. Jellies take longer to make, as time has to be allowed for the fruit juice to drip through the jelly bag.

If possible, use fruits that have a good pectin content and, if necessary, add other fruits that will increase this content.

jellies

Cook the fruits in water, remembering that the riper the fruits, the less water required. Do ensure that the cooking process is slow, as the longer the cooking, the greater the yield of juice. With jelly-making, it is quite difficult to give an exact yield, as this depends on the ripeness of fruits and the amount of juice extracted. After boiling, remove any scum with a slotted spoon, then pot in the usual way.

Cranberry jelly

MAKES about 2 lb 4 oz/1 kg

2 lb/900 g fresh cranberries, washed

2 large oranges (preferably unwaxed and organic), scrubbed and cut into wedges

1 lemon (preferably unwaxed and organic), scrubbed and cut into wedges

3½ cups water

about 1 lb/450 g sugar (see method)

Place the cranberries, oranges, and lemon in a large pan. Add the water bring to a boil, then reduce the heat and simmer for 45 minutes, or until the cranberries are very soft and pulpy. Strain through a jelly bag.

Once all the juice has been extracted, measure, then return to the rinsed-out pan. Add the sugar, allowing 1 lb/450 g of sugar for every 2½ cups of juice. Heat gently, stirring frequently, until the sugar has completely dissolved. Bring to a boil and boil rapidly for 15 minutes, or until the setting point is reached.

Let cool slightly and skim if necessary. Pot into warmed sterilized jars and cover the tops with wax disks. When completely cold, cover with cellophane or lids, then label and store in a cool place.

Cook's tip: Add 2–3 whole cloves when simmering the fruits for a spicy flavor.

Pineapple and mint jelly

MAKES about 2 lb 4 oz/1 kg

1 large ripe pineapple, about
1 lb 12 oz/800 g (peeled weight)

2 tart cooking apples, about
1 lb/450 g (total weight)

5 cups water

few fresh mint sprigs

about 1 lb 8 oz/675 g sugar
(see method)

2 tbsp chopped fresh mint

green food coloring (optional)

Peel the pineapple and cut lengthwise into 4 wedges. Chop the pineapple, including the core, into small chunks and place in a large pan. Chop the apples (do not peel or core) and add to the pan with the water and mint sprigs. Bring to a boil, then reduce the heat and simmer for 1 hour, or until the fruits are very soft. Let cool slightly before straining through a jelly bag.

Once all the juice has been extracted, measure, then return to the rinsed-out pan. Add the sugar, allowing 1 lb/450 g of sugar for every 2½ cups of juice. Heat gently, stirring frequently, until the sugar has completely dissolved. Bring to a boil and boil rapidly for 10–15 minutes, or until the setting point is reached.

Remove and let cool for at least 5 minutes. Skim, if necessary, then stir in the chopped mint and green food coloring (if using). Pot into warmed sterilized jars and cover the tops with wax disks. When completely cold, cover with cellophane or lids, then label and store in a cool place.

Cook's tip: Replace the mint with a few sprigs of fresh rosemary or basil. This is perfect for serving with meat dishes.

Rhubarb and strawberry jelly

Place the rhubarb in a large pan with the water, strawberries, and ginger and simmer over gentle heat for 1 hour, or until the fruits are very soft and pulpy. Strain through a jelly bag.

Once all the juice has been extracted, measure, then return to the rinsed-out pan. Add the sugar, allowing 1 lb/450 g of sugar for every 2½ cups of juice. Heat gently, stirring frequently, until the sugar has completely dissolved, then bring to a boil and boil rapidly for 10–15 minutes, or until the setting point is reached.

Cool slightly and skim, if necessary, then pot into warmed sterilized jars and cover the tops with wax disks. When completely cold, cover with cellophane or lids, then label and store in a cool place.

Cook's tip: Once the jars have been filled, avoid moving the jelly too much, as a lot of movement at this stage might affect the setting quality.

MAKES about 3 lb 14 oz/1.75 kg

1 lb 8 oz/675 g fresh rhubarb, trimmed, washed, and cut into short lengths

5 cups water

2 lb/900 g strawberries, hulled and rinsed

2-inch/5-cm piece gingerroot, peeled and chopped

about 2 lb/900 g sugar (see method)

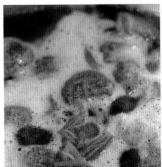

Bell pepper and chile jelly

MAKES about 1 lb 8 oz/675 g

3–5 serrano red chiles,
or according to taste

8 red bell peppers, seeded and
coarsely chopped

2 tart cooking apples, washed and
coarsely chopped

²/₃ cup white wine vinegar

6¹/₂ cups water

1 tbsp coriander seeds,
lightly crushed

2-inch/5-cm piece fresh gingerroot,
peeled and grated

about 2 lb/900 g sugar
(see method)

1 cup liquid pectin

Cut 2–3 chiles in half, then discard the seeds and chop the flesh. Place the chiles, bell peppers, and apples in a large pan with the vinegar, water, coriander seeds, and ginger. Bring to a boil, then reduce the heat and simmer for 1 hour, or until the bell peppers are very tender. Strain through a jelly bag.

Once all the liquid has been extracted, measure, then return to the rinsed-out pan. Add the sugar, allowing 1 lb/450 g of sugar for every 2¹/₂ cups of pepper juice. Discard the seeds from 1–2 of the remaining chiles and set aside. (The other chile could be used if a very hot jelly is preferred.) Heat gently, stirring frequently, until the sugar has completely dissolved, then bring to a boil and boil rapidly for 3 minutes, or until the setting point is reached.

Let cool for 5 minutes. Skim, then stir in the pectin and the reserved chopped chiles. Pot into warmed sterilized jars and cover the tops with wax disks. When completely cold, cover with cellophane or lids, then label and store in a cool place.

Cook's tip: Take care when handling chiles: avoid touching your eyes or any other sensitive parts of the body until the hands have been thoroughly washed.

Wine jelly

MAKES about 1 lb 8 oz/675 g

1 lb/450 g tart cooking apples, washed and cut into chunks

2¹⁄₂ cups water

1 bottle red wine, such as claret

about 1 lb 8 oz/675 g sugar (see method)

Place the apples in a large pan together with the water and wine. Bring to a boil, then reduce the heat and simmer for 30 minutes, or until the apples are very soft and pulpy. Strain through a jelly bag.

Once all the juice has been extracted, measure, then return to the rinsed-out pan. Add the sugar, allowing 1 lb/450 g of sugar for every 2¹⁄₂ cups of juice. Heat gently, stirring frequently, until the sugar has completely dissolved. Bring to a boil and boil rapidly for 15 minutes, or until the setting point is reached.

Let cool slightly. Skim, then pot into warmed sterilized jars and cover the tops with wax disks. When completely cold, cover with cellophane or lids, then label and store in a cool place.

Cook's tip: Other wines, such as white or rosé, can be used as well.

Tomato jelly

Place the 2 lb/900 g tomatoes in a large pan. Chop the orange and add to the pan. Lightly bruise the lemongrass and add to the pan with the ginger, star anise, whole cloves, water, and vinegar. Place over gentle heat, then cover and simmer for 40–50 minutes, or until the tomatoes are very soft and pulpy. Let cool slightly before straining through a jelly bag.

Once all the juice has been extracted, measure, then return to the rinsed-out pan. Add the sugar, allowing 1 lb/450 g of sugar for every 2½ cups of juice. Heat gently, stirring frequently, until the sugar has completely dissolved, then stir in the tomato paste. Bring to a boil and boil rapidly for 10–20 minutes, or until the setting point is reached.

Let cool for at least 5 minutes, then skim before stirring in the 2 seeded chopped tomatoes. Pot into warmed sterilized jars and cover the tops with wax disks. When completely cold, cover with cellophane or lids, then label and store in a cool place.

Cook's tip: If liked, 2 tablespoons of chopped fresh cilantro can be added to the finished jelly with the two chopped tomatoes.

MAKES about 3 lb/1.3 kg

2 lb/900 g unblemished firm, ripe tomatoes, rinsed and chopped

1 large orange (preferably unwaxed and organic), unpeeled and scrubbed

2 lemongrass stalks, coarsely chopped

2-inch/5-cm piece fresh gingerroot, peeled and chopped

1–2 whole star anise

3 whole cloves

3½ cups water

3 tbsp white wine vinegar

about 2 lb/900 g sugar (see method)

2 tbsp tomato paste

2 firm, ripe tomatoes, seeded and chopped

Making marmalade is very similar to the process of jam-making, but there are a few differences. Marmalade is normally made with Seville oranges (sour oranges), which are specially grown fruits that are bitter and not suitable for eating raw. They will freeze well, which is good because they are available only at the end of January and early February. Wash and dry thoroughly before freezing and thaw completely before using. Sweet oranges can be used with other citrus fruits if Seville oranges are not available.

marmalade

As citrus peel is tough, it either needs presoaking or cooking before use. It is also advisable to peel the fruits with a vegetable peeler to remove all of the bitter white pith.

As the cooking time is much longer, more water is required to allow for evaporation. The contents of the pan need to be reduced by half before the sugar is added. Failure to do this is one of the reasons for a marmalade not setting. Try experimenting by adding different spices or fruits to the basic recipe, and discover some delicious new flavors.

Traditional chunky marmalade

MAKES about 10 lb/4.5 kg

3 lb 5 oz/1.5 kg Seville
oranges, scrubbed

juice from 2 large lemons

6 quarts water

6 lb/2.7 kg sugar

Cut the oranges in half and squeeze out all the juice. Scoop out all the seeds from the orange shells and tie up in a small piece of cheesecloth. Slice the peel into small chunks or strips and place in a large pan together with the orange and lemon juice and water. Add the bag of seeds.

Simmer gently for 1½ hours, or until the peel is very soft and the liquid has reduced by half. Remove the bag of seeds, carefully squeezing to remove any juice. Add the sugar and heat, stirring, until the sugar has completely dissolved. Bring to a boil and boil rapidly for about 15 minutes, or until the setting point is reached.

Let cool slightly, then pot into warmed sterilized jars and cover the tops with wax disks. When completely cold, cover with cellophane or lids, then label and store in a cool place.

Cook's tip: Seville oranges freeze well, so if you don't have time to make a year's supply of marmalade, buy the oranges when they are in season and freeze for use later in the year.

Ginger citrus marmalade

MAKES about 3 lb/1.3 kg

4 limes (preferably unwaxed and organic), scrubbed

2 large lemons (preferably unwaxed and organic), scrubbed

small piece fresh gingerroot, peeled and chopped

5 cups water

2 tsp ground ginger

about 2 lb/900 g sugar (see method)

4 oz/115 g preserved ginger, chopped

Cut off and discard both ends from the limes and lemons and wash thoroughly. Place in a large pan together with the chopped gingerroot and the water, then bring to a boil. Reduce the heat, then cover with a tight-fitting lid and simmer for 1½ hours, or until the fruits are very soft.

Cool slightly, then drain off the liquid and set aside. Chop the fruits as finely as possible, discarding the seeds.

Return the chopped fruits to the rinsed-out pan together with the reserved liquid and the ground ginger. Add the sugar, allowing 1 lb/450 g of sugar for every 2½ cups of liquid. Heat gently, stirring frequently, until the sugar has completely dissolved. Bring to a boil and boil rapidly for about 15 minutes, or until the setting point is reached.

Let cool for 5 minutes, then stir in the preserved ginger. Pot into warmed sterilized jars and cover the tops with wax disks. When completely cold, cover with cellophane or lids, then label and store in a cool place.

Cook's tip: If the limes and lemons are waxed, scrub vigorously to remove the wax coating.

Lemon and orange marmalade

Before cooking, peel half the fruits very thinly, taking care not to include the bitter white pith, and cut into very fine shreds. Place in a small pan, then cover with water and simmer for 30 minutes, or until soft. Drain and set aside.

Cut all the fruits into small wedges and place in a large pan with any seeds and the water, then bring to a boil. Reduce the heat, then cover and simmer for about 1½ hours, or until very soft.

Let cool slightly, then strain through a jelly bag. Measure the strained juice and return to the pan, adding 1 lb/450 g of sugar for every 2½ cups of liquid. Heat gently, stirring frequently, until the sugar has completely dissolved. Bring to a boil and boil rapidly for 15 minutes, or until the setting point is reached.

Let cool slightly, then stir in the reserved shredded peel. Pot into warmed sterilized jars and cover the tops with wax disks. When completely cold, cover with cellophane or lids, then label and store in a cool place.

Cook's tip: If liked, the fruit peel can be chopped after simmering in the water, with a very sharp cook's knife or vegetable cleaver.

MAKES about 4 lb/1.8 kg

3 lb 5 oz/1.5 kg lemons and oranges (preferably unwaxed and organic), scrubbed

3½ cups water

about 2 lb/900 g sugar (see method)

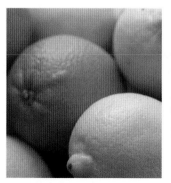

Reduced sugar marmalade

MAKES about 5 lb/2.25 kg

3 lb 5 oz/1.5 kg oranges
(preferably unwaxed and organic),
washed or scrubbed

1 lb/450 g mandarins (preferably
unwaxed and organic), scrubbed

7 cups water

2 lb 12 oz/1.25 kg sugar

Using a vegetable peeler, remove the peel as thinly as possible from 1 lb 8 oz/675 g of the oranges and 8 oz/225 g of the mandarins, then cut the peel into fine shreds. Place in a small pan, then cover with water and simmer for 30 minutes, or until soft. Drain and set aside.

Peel the remaining oranges and mandarins and cut all the fruits in half, discarding the bitter white pith from them. Reserve the seeds and tie up in a piece of cheesecloth together with the rest of the peel. Cut the fruit flesh into chunks and place in a large pan together with the water and the bag of seeds and peel.

Bring to a boil. Reduce the heat, then cover and simmer gently for 1 hour, or until the fruits are very soft. Remove the cheesecloth bag and discard. Add the sugar and heat gently, stirring frequently, until the sugar has completely dissolved. Bring to a boil and boil rapidly for 15 minutes, or until the setting point is reached.

Let cool for 5–8 minutes, then stir in the reserved shredded peel. Pot into warmed sterilized jars and cover the tops with wax disks. When completely cold, cover with cellophane or lids, then label and store in a cool place.

Cook's tip: Other citrus fruits can be used in this recipe, such as grapefruits, limes, clementines, and Seville oranges.

  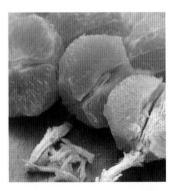

Orange and squash marmalade

MAKES about 5 lb/2.25 kg

2 lb/900 g acorn or butternut squash (peeled and seeded weight), cut into small chunks

6 blood oranges, scrubbed

²/₃ cup freshly squeezed lemon juice

small piece fresh gingerroot, peeled and grated

2 serrano chiles, seeded and finely sliced

5 cups water

2 lb 12 oz/1.25 kg sugar

Place the squash in a large pan with a tight-fitting lid. Thinly slice 2 of the oranges without peeling, reserving the seeds, and add to the pan. Peel the remaining oranges and chop the flesh, then add to the pan together with the lemon juice, grated ginger, and sliced chiles. Tie the orange seeds up in a piece of cheesecloth and add to the pan with the water.

Bring to a boil. Reduce the heat, then cover and simmer gently for 1 hour, or until the squash and oranges are very soft. Remove the seeds and discard.

Add the sugar and heat gently, stirring, until the sugar has completely dissolved. Bring to a boil and boil rapidly for 15 minutes, or until the setting point is reached.

Skim if necessary, then let cool for 10 minutes. Pot into warmed sterilized jars and cover the tops with wax disks. When completely cold, cover with cellophane or lids, then label, and store in a cool place.

Cook's tip: This is ideal to serve with meat and cheese dishes. If liked, heat gently before serving.

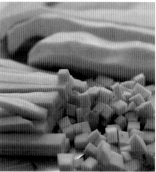

Orange and kiwi marmalade

Peel the oranges as thinly as possible and set aside the peel. Cut the fruits in half and squeeze out all the juice. Scoop out the seeds and tie the seeds up in a small piece of cheesecloth together with the chopped ginger. Finely shred the orange peel and place in a large pan. Add the kiwifruit to the pan together with the water, orange juice, and seeds.

Bring to a boil, then reduce the heat and simmer gently for 1 hour, or until the peel and fruits are very soft. Remove the seeds and discard.

Add the sugar and heat gently, stirring frequently, until the sugar has completely dissolved. Add the butter. Bring to a boil and boil rapidly for about 15 minutes, or until the setting point is reached.

Let cool slightly, then pot into warm sterilized jars and cover the tops with wax disks. When completely cold, cover with cellophane or lids, then label and store in a cool place.

Cook's tip: If liked, add a little finely chopped preserved ginger to the pan once the setting point is reached and the marmalade has cooled and is ready to pot.

MAKES about 2 lb/900 g

3 lb 5 oz/1.5 kg oranges (preferably unwaxed and organic), washed

2-inch/5-cm piece fresh gingerroot, peeled and chopped

6 kiwifruit, peeled and finely chopped

7 cups water

4 lb/1.8 kg sugar

1 tsp butter

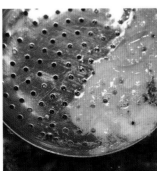

Curds and butters are a traditional way of preserving fruits, and were originally made when there was a glut of produce.

Curds contain eggs and sugar with the rind and juice of a fruit, and are cooked slowly over a pan of gently simmering water until the eggs are thoroughly cooked and the mixture thick and creamy. These keep well unopened, but once opened they should be kept in the refrigerator and used within a month.

curds and butters

Butters do not keep very long and are normally made from pitted fruits, apples, quince, and black currants. In spite of the name, they do not contain any butter. They should be cooked to a thick cream and used as you would for lemon curd.

Traditional lemon curd

MAKES about 1 lb 8 oz/675 g

4 lemons (preferably unwaxed and organic), scrubbed and dried

4 eggs, beaten

8 tbsp unsalted butter, diced

1 lb/450 g granulated sugar   3.5 cups

Finely grate the rind from the lemons and squeeze out all the juice. Place the rind and juice in a heatproof bowl, then stir in the eggs and add the butter and sugar.

Place over a pan of gently simmering water, ensuring that the bottom of the bowl does not touch the water. Cook, stirring constantly, until the sugar has completely dissolved, then continue to cook, stirring frequently, until the mixture thickens and coats the back of the spoon.

Spoon into warmed sterilized jars and cover the tops with wax disks. When completely cold, cover with lids, then label and store in a cool, dark place. Use within 3 months and once opened, store in the refrigerator.

Cook's tip: Other fruits can be used in this recipe. Try orange or lime or even a mixture of all three. Add the flesh and seeds of a ripe passion fruit to the mixture when adding the sugar.

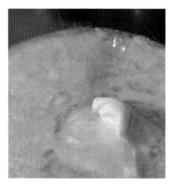

Apple butter

MAKES about 2 lb 4 oz/1 kg

3 lb 5 oz/1.5 kg tart cooking apples, washed

5 cups sweet cider or apple juice

²/₃ cup water

²/₃ cup lemon juice

2 tbsp grated lemon rind

2 cinnamon sticks, lightly bruised

about 1 lb/450 g granulated sugar (see method)

Chop the apples into small chunks (do not peel or core), discarding any damaged pieces. Place in a large pan together with the cider or apple juice, water, lemon juice, lemon rind, and cinnamon sticks. Bring to a boil, then reduce the heat and simmer gently for 30 minutes, stirring occasionally, until the apples have completely collapsed. Remove and discard the cinnamon sticks.

Strain the mixture, then measure the apple pulp and return to the rinsed-out pan. Add the sugar; allow 1¾ cups to each 2½ cups of pulp. Heat gently, stirring constantly, until the sugar has completely dissolved. Continue to cook for an additional 15–20 minutes, or until a thick creamy consistency is achieved.

Pot into warmed sterilized jars and cover the tops with wax disks. When completely cold, cover with lids, then label and store in a cool, dark place.

Cook's tips: Store in a cool, dark place for up to 3 months. Once opened, keep in the refrigerator for up to 10 days. If liked, crab apples or windfall apples can be used in place of the cooking apples, and the cinnamon can be replaced with fresh gingerroot. If using crab apples, simmer for at least 1 hour, or until soft, then strain and proceed as in the main recipe.

Plum butter

Place the plums in a large pan with the water and bring to a boil. Reduce the heat and simmer gently for 40–50 minutes, or until the plums are very soft and have collapsed. Let cool, then strain and measure the pulp in a measuring cup or pitcher. Return to the rinsed-out pan.

Add the orange rind and juice with the cinnamon and heat gently for 10 minutes. Stir in the sugar, allowing 1¾ cups to each 2½ cups of pulp. Heat gently, stirring frequently, until the sugar has completely dissolved. Bring to a boil, then boil gently until the mixture has thickened and is creamy.

Pot into warmed sterilized jars and cover the tops with wax disks. When completely cold, cover with lids, then label. Store in a cool, dark place and use within 3 months of making. Once opened, store in the refrigerator and use within 2 weeks of opening.

Cook's tip: Add a few sprigs of fresh rosemary or thyme and sage when first cooking the plums, and discard when straining. This is ideal to serve with both hot and cold meat dishes.

MAKES about 1 lb 8 oz/675 g

3 lb 5 oz/1.5 kg ripe plums, washed and cut in half, pits discarded

2½ cups water

2 tbsp grated orange rind

1¼ cups freshly squeezed orange juice

1½ tsp ground cinnamon

about 2 lb/900 g granulated sugar (see method)

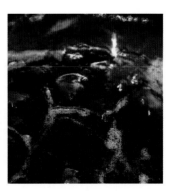

Apple and orange curd

MAKES about 1 lb 8 oz/675 g

1 lb/450 g tart cooking apples, peeled, cored, and chopped

$^2/_3$ cup water

2 large oranges (preferably unwaxed and organic), scrubbed

2 eggs, beaten

8 tbsp unsalted butter, diced

generous $^1/_2$ cup superfine sugar

3–4 whole cloves

Place the apples and water in a large pan and cook for 10–12 minutes, or until soft and fluffy. Remove from the heat and beat until smooth, then strain. Place the fruit pulp in a heatproof bowl set over a pan of gently simmering water.

Finely grate the rind from one of the oranges and squeeze out the juice from both oranges to give $^2/_3$ cup juice. Add to the bowl together with the eggs, butter, sugar, and cloves. Cook, stirring frequently, until the butter and sugar have melted.

Continue to cook, stirring, until the mixture becomes thick and creamy. Remove the cloves and discard. Pot into warmed sterilized jars and cover the tops with wax disks. When completely cold, cover with lids, then label and store in a cool, dark place.

Cook's tip: Try using other citrus fruits and replace the cloves with cinnamon, star anise, or the ripe seeds and juice from 2 passion fruits.

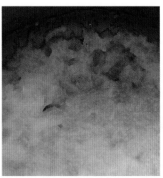

Apricot and passion fruit butter

MAKES about 2 lb/900 g

1 lb 8 oz/675 g fresh ripe apricots, washed and pitted

juice from 2 large oranges to give ²/₃ cup liquid

2¹/₂ cups water

1 tsp ground allspice

3 ripe passion fruits

scant 1 cup granulated sugar, or to taste

Place the apricots in a large pan and add the orange juice and water. Bring to a boil. Reduce the heat to a simmer, then cover with a tight-fitting lid and cook for 45 minutes, or until the apricots have collapsed and are very soft. During cooking, check the liquid has not evaporated. If so, reduce the heat and add a little more water if necessary. Let cool slightly, then strain.

Return the strained apricot pulp to a large pan. Add the ground allspice with the seeds and flesh from the passion fruits and scant 1 cup sugar. Heat gently, stirring frequently, until the sugar has completely dissolved. Increase the heat slightly and continue to cook, stirring frequently, until thick and creamy. Adjust the sweetness to taste and cook for a little longer if more sugar has been added.

Let cool for 5 minutes, then spoon into warmed sterilized jars and cover the tops with wax disks. When completely cold, cover with lids, then label and store in a cool, dark place.

Cook's tip: Other fruits can be used in place of the apricots. Try dried mango, papaya, or dried fruit salad.

Chutneys, pickles, and relishes are the perfect way to ensure that gluts of homegrown vegetables are never wasted. Use wide-necked jars when making chutneys, pickles, and relishes to enable you to fit in larger pieces of the vegetables.

Chutneys and relishes are made using an assortment of vegetables and spices with the addition of fruit, fresh or dried, with sugar and vinegar used as a preservative. Chutneys are best if left to mature for two to four weeks before using.

chutneys, pickles, and relishes

Relishes are perhaps a more modern way of preserving fruits and vegetables, offering a slightly fresher feel to the meal as they do not need a long cooking period. Relishes do not need to stand before using and most can be cooked and served the same day.

Pickles are made from crisp, fresh vegetables and are soaked in brine (water and salt, either table or cooking salt) first of all. The vegetables must be thoroughly rinsed before proceeding with the recipe to ensure that the brine is removed, otherwise the result will have a very salty taste. They are then combined with vinegars, flavorings, and sugar.

Fruity apple chutney

MAKES about 7 lb 10 oz/3.5 kg

2 lb/900 g tart cooking apples, peeled, cored, and chopped

1 lb/450 g onions, chopped

1 lb/450 g ripe plums, rinsed, pitted, and chopped

rind and juice of 2 lemons (preferably unwaxed and organic), scrubbed

2¼ cups fresh cranberries (if fresh are unavailable, use dried)

1 lb/450 g brown sugar

4 kiwifruit, peeled and sliced

2 cups vinegar

2 tbsp balsamic vinegar

Place the apples, onions, and plums in a large pan with the lemon rind, juice, and cranberries. Cook over gentle heat, stirring frequently, for 12 minutes, or until the cranberries are beginning to "pop."

Stir in all the remaining ingredients and heat gently, stirring occasionally, until the sugar has completely dissolved. Bring to a boil, then reduce the heat and simmer for 35–40 minutes, or until a thick consistency is reached.

Remove from the heat and let cool slightly, then pot into warmed sterilized jars. Cover with nonmetallic lids, then label and store in a cool place.

Cook's tip: When making chutney or pickle, do remember to use stainless steel, enamel, or aluminum pans. Vinegar can impart a metallic taste if a copper or iron pan is used.

Banana, mango, and date chutney

MAKES about 7 lb 10 oz/3.5 kg

1 lb/450 g tart cooking apples,
peeled, cored, and chopped

2–3 large mangos, about 1 lb/
450 g (peeled weight), chopped

12 oz/350 g onions, chopped

3–4 garlic cloves, chopped

1 red serrano chile, seeded
and chopped

6 large ripe but firm bananas,
chopped

1³/₄ cups brown sugar

2 cups unsweetened
chopped dates

2 tsp ground cinnamon

2¹/₂–3 cups vinegar

Place all the ingredients in a large pan and cook over gentle heat, stirring frequently, until the sugar has completely dissolved.

Bring to a boil, then reduce the heat and simmer for 45 minutes, or until a thick chutney consistency is reached. Add extra vinegar during simmering if becoming dry.

Remove from the heat and let cool slightly, then pot into warmed sterilized jars. Cover with nonmetallic lids, then label and store in a cool place.

Cook's tip: Do not use very soft bananas because the finished chutney will not have a good consistency and will be slightly mushy.

Tomato chutney

Place the tomatoes, apples, onions, celery, chile, and sugar in a large pan. Tie the coriander seeds in a small piece of cheesecloth, then add to the pan together with the water and cook over gentle heat, stirring occasionally, for 30 minutes, or until the tomatoes and apples have collapsed.

Add both vinegars and the golden raisins and bring to a boil, then reduce the heat and simmer for 35–45 minutes, or until a thick consistency is reached.

Let cool slightly and discard the coriander seeds, then pot into warmed sterilized jars. Cover with nonmetallic lids, then label and store in a cool place.

Cook's tip: Green tomatoes can also be used for this chutney recipe, if liked. Replace the coriander seeds with fresh gingerroot.

MAKES about 7 lb 10 oz/3.5 kg

3 lb 5 oz/1.5 kg firm ripe tomatoes, washed and chopped

1 lb/450 g tart cooking apples, peeled, cored, and chopped

1 lb/450 g red onions, chopped

1 head of celery, trimmed and chopped, leaves discarded

1 green jalapeño chile, seeded and chopped

1 lb 8 oz/675 g turbinado sugar

1 tsp coriander seeds, lightly pounded

$^2/_3$ cup water

$2^1/_2$ cups vinegar

4 tbsp balsamic vinegar

$1^3/_4$ cups golden raisins

Mixed vegetable pickle

MAKES about 6 lb/2.75 kg

4 lb 8 oz/2 kg mixed vegetables, such as cauliflower, carrots, baby onions, celery, and cucumber, chopped into small pieces

6 garlic cloves, chopped

$^2/_3$ cup salt

5 cups boiling water

$1^1/_8$ cups granulated sugar

1 tbsp mustard powder

1 tbsp ground turmeric

5 cups vinegar

2-inch/5-cm piece fresh gingerroot, peeled and grated

3 tbsp all-purpose flour

Place the vegetables and garlic in a large bowl. In another bowl, dissolve the salt in the boiling water and pour over the vegetables. Cover and leave for 24 hours.

The next day, drain the vegetables thoroughly and rinse in cold water. Drain again and place in a large pan and set aside. Mix the sugar with the mustard powder and turmeric, then mix in half the vinegar. Pour over the vegetables, then stir in the grated ginger and bring to a boil. Reduce the heat and simmer for 20 minutes, or until the vegetables are tender but still retain a bite.

Blend the flour with the remaining vinegar and stir into the vegetables. Cook, stirring, for 5 minutes, or until the liquid thickens.

Remove from the heat and let cool for 5 minutes before potting into warmed sterilized jars. Cover with nonmetallic lids, then label and store in a cool place.

Cook's tip: For a milder pickle, omit the mustard and turmeric and add 1 tablespoon ground cinnamon with 2 teaspoons allspice and 1 teaspoon ground cloves.

Pear, cranberry, and celery root relish

MAKES about 5 lb/2.25 kg

1$\frac{1}{8}$ cups turbinado sugar

1$\frac{1}{4}$ cups white wine vinegar

2$\frac{1}{2}$ cups water

2 lb/900 g firm but almost ripe pears, peeled, cored, and chopped

1 large celery root, about 1 lb/ 450 g, peeled and finely chopped

8 oz/225 g carrots, grated

1 lb/450 g onions, finely chopped

2-inch/5-cm piece fresh gingerroot

2 cinnamon sticks, lightly bruised

1$\frac{1}{4}$ cups dried cranberries

Place the sugar, vinegar, and water in a large, nonreactive pan and simmer gently until the sugar has completely dissolved. Add the pears and celery root to the pan with the grated carrots and onions.

Tie the gingerroot and cinnamon sticks in a piece of cheesecloth and add to the pan. Simmer the fruit and vegetables for 30 minutes, then add the dried cranberries and continue to simmer for an additional 20 minutes, or until a thickened consistency is formed.

Let cool slightly, then pot into warmed sterilized jars. Cover with nonmetallic lids, then label and store in a cool place.

Cook's tip: If fresh cranberries are available, add to the pan at the beginning of cooking the pears and celery root.

Blueberry relish

Place the blueberries, apples, onions, bell peppers, and rosemary sprigs in a large, nonreactive pan. Stir in the sugar (add the minimum and add more according to taste later) with the white wine vinegar. Bring to a boil. Reduce the heat, then cover and simmer for 30 minutes, or until a thickened consistency is achieved. Add a little water if the liquid has evaporated and reduce the heat, if necessary.

Remove the rosemary sprigs and stir in the balsamic vinegar. Cook for an additional 5 minutes.

Let cool slightly before potting into warmed sterilized jars. Cover with nonmetallic lids, then label and store in a cool place.

Cook's tip: Other fruits can be added to the relish if liked. Try chopped, no-soak dried figs or fresh cranberries (you may need a little extra sugar if using fresh cranberries).

MAKES about 3 lb/1.3 kg

2 lb/900 g fresh blueberries, rinsed

2 large tart cooking apples, peeled, cored, and finely chopped

10 oz/300 g onions, finely chopped

1 large or 2 small red bell peppers, seeded and chopped

2–3 fresh rosemary sprigs

1^1/$_8$–1^3/$_4$ cups light brown sugar, or to taste

1^1/$_4$ cups white wine vinegar

3 tbsp balsamic vinegar

Melon rind pickle

MAKES about 2 lb/900 g

1 lb/450 g melon rind, chopped
into small pieces

2 tbsp salt

2½ cups very hot water,
plus an extra 3½ cups

1 lb/450 g turbinado sugar

3 whole star anise

6 cardamom pods, lightly cracked

2 whole cloves

1¾ cups dried apricots,
finely chopped

Place the rind in a large, nonreactive pan. In a heatproof bowl, dissolve the salt in the 2½ cups water and pour over the melon rind. Cover and let stand for 30 minutes.

Bring the melon rind to a boil and simmer for 30 minutes. Drain and rinse, then return to the pan and cover with the remaining water. Bring to a boil and simmer for 10 minutes. Drain, then cover with fresh water. Bring to a boil and boil again for 10 minutes. Remove from the heat and leave overnight.

The next day, drain the melon rind and return to the large, nonreactive pan. Add the sugar, together with the spices, tied up in a small piece of cheesecloth, and the apricots.

Simmer over gentle heat for 1 hour, or until the melon rind is clear. Remove the spices and pot into warmed sterilized jars. Cover with nonmetallic lids, then label and store in a cool place.

Cook's tip: If liked, a little green food coloring can be added at the end of cooking.

Fruits and vegetables have been preserved for centuries and play an important part in many cuisines. The term "preserve" is used to describe fruits or vegetables that have been cooked with sugar and/or vinegar so they can be kept for a long period of time. They are potted in sterilized, sealed jars and kept, preferably, in a cool, dark cupboard. It is important that the fruits and vegetables are ripe but not mushy, and as fresh as possible. It is possible to use slightly damaged or bruised produce as long as the bruised parts are discarded.

preserves

The recipes in this chapter are designed to be used with hot and cold dishes, to either complement a dish or to give a tang or hint of sweetness.

Sweet mango preserve

MAKES about 3 lb 5 oz/1.5 kg

4 ripe mangos, about 2 lb/900 g, peeled and finely chopped

1–2 red chiles, seeded and chopped

2-inch/5-cm piece fresh gingerroot, peeled and grated

grated rind and juice of 2 lemons (preferably unwaxed and organic), scrubbed

2 1/2 cups water

1 lb/450 g light brown sugar

1 cup golden raisins

2–3 tbsp balsamic vinegar

Place the mangos, chiles, and ginger in a large pan. Add the lemon rind and juice and stir in the water. Bring to a boil and simmer for 20 minutes.

Add the sugar and heat gently until the sugar has completely dissolved. Bring to a boil and boil for 10 minutes, or until a thick consistency is reached. Stir in the golden raisins and balsamic vinegar and cook for an additional 5 minutes.

Let cool slightly. Pot into warmed sterilized jars and cover the tops with wax disks. When completely cold, cover with cellophane or lids, then label and store in a cool place.

Cook's tip: Other flavors can be used instead of the chiles and gingerroot, if liked. Try adding 2 vanilla beans, or 4 star anise, 6 lightly cracked cardamom pods, and 2 whole cloves, tied in a small piece of cheesecloth. Remove before potting.

Sweet beet preserve

MAKES about 5 lb/2.25 kg

2 lb/900 g raw beet, peeled and grated or finely chopped

8 oz/225 g onions, finely chopped

1 lb/450 g tart cooking apples, peeled, cored, and finely chopped

grated rind and juice of 2 large oranges (preferably unwaxed and organic), scrubbed

3 1/2 cups vinegar

1 1/4 cups water

1 lb/450 g turbinado sugar

generous 1 1/3 cups seedless raisins

Place the beet in a large pan with the onions, apples, orange rind, and juice. Add the vinegar and water and bring to a boil. Reduce the heat and simmer for 15 minutes.

Add the sugar and heat gently, stirring frequently, until the sugar has completely dissolved, then stir in the raisins. Simmer for an additional 30 minutes, or until the beet is soft.

Let cool slightly. Pot into warmed sterilized jars and cover the tops with wax disks. When completely cold, cover with cellophane or lids, then label and store in a cool place.

Cook's tip: If preferred, replace the raisins with an equal quantity of canned cherries or chopped maraschino cherries.

Berry preserve

Place all the fruits in a large pan with the lemon juice and sugar. Heat gently, stirring occasionally, until the sugar has completely dissolved. Add the butter.

Bring to a boil and boil rapidly for 3 minutes, then remove from the heat and stir in the pectin. Let cool before skimming. Pot into warmed sterilized jars and cover the tops with wax disks. When completely cold, cover with cellophane or lids, then label and store in a cool place.

Cook's tip: Make sure that the fruits are undamaged and free from blemishes.

MAKES about 4 lb/1.8 kg

2 lb/900 g assorted berries, such as blueberries, cranberries, raspberries, and strawberries, hulled and rinsed

3 tbsp lemon juice

2 lb/900 g granulated sugar

1 tsp butter

1 cup liquid pectin

Raspberry and apple preserve

MAKES about 2 lb/900 g

1 lb 5 oz/600 g tart cooking apples, peeled, cored, and chopped

1 lb 5 oz/600 g fresh ripe raspberries, rinsed

1 cup lemon juice

1 lb/450 g granulated sugar

1 cup liquid pectin

Layer all the fruits with the lemon juice, sugar, and pectin in a large clean mixing bowl. Cover tightly and leave overnight.

The next day, stir well and pour the mixture into a large pan. Bring to a boil, stirring occasionally, and boil for 4 minutes. Remove from the heat and let cool for 5 minutes.

Pot into warmed sterilized jars and cover the tops with wax disks. When completely cold, cover with cellophane or lids, then label and store in a cool place. Once opened, store in the refrigerator and use within 10 days.

Cook's tips: Other berries can be used in place of the raspberries. Try blackberries with orange in place of the lemon juice.

Pepper pot preserve

MAKES about 3 lb/1.3 kg

1 lb/450 g tart cooking apples, peeled, cored, and chopped

1 lb/450 g onions, thinly sliced

3–4 garlic cloves, sliced

2–4 serrano chiles, seeded and finely sliced

2 lb/900 g assorted colored bell peppers, seeded and finely chopped

1 lb/450 g turbinado sugar, or add a little extra if a sweeter relish is preferred

1–3 tsp Tabasco sauce, or to taste

1¼ cups red wine vinegar

⅓ cup balsamic vinegar

Place the apples in a large pan together with the onions, garlic, chiles, and bell peppers. Sprinkle with the sugar, then add the Tabasco sauce. Simmer over gentle heat for 15 minutes, stirring frequently, until the apples and onions are beginning to soften.

Add the vinegars and continue to simmer for 40 minutes, or until a thick consistency is reached and the liquid is absorbed. Check the sweetness and if necessary add a little extra sugar, then simmer for an additional 10 minutes.

Remove from the heat and let cool for 5 minutes. Pot into warmed sterilized jars and cover the tops with wax disks. When completely cold, cover with cellophane or lids, then label and store in a cool place.

Cook's tip: If a more fiery relish is preferred, use hotter chiles such as Thai chile or habañero.

index

apple
    apple butter 60
    apple and orange curd 64
    fruity apple chutney 70
    pepper pot preserve 94
    raspberry and apple preserve 92
    wine jelly 38
apricot
    apricot and passion fruit butter 66
    quick apricot jam 25

banana
    banana, mango, and date chutney 72
beet
    sweet beet preserve 88
bell pepper
    bell pepper and chile jelly 36
    pepper pot preserve 94
blueberry
    berry preserve 91
    blueberry relish 81
    spicy blueberry jam 16
butters
    apple butter 60
    apricot and passion fruit butter 66
    plum butter 63

celery root
    pear, cranberry, and celery root relish 78
cherry
    cherry with brandy jam 19
chutney
    banana, mango, and date chutney 72
    fruity apple chutney 70
    tomato chutney 75
cranberry
    berry preserve 91
    cranberry jelly 30
    pear, cranberry, and celery root relish 78
curds
    apple and orange curd 64
    traditional lemon curd 58

date
    banana, mango, and date chutney 72

ginger
    ginger citrus marmalade 46
    melon and ginger jam 26
jam
    cherry with brandy jam 19
    classic strawberry jam 14
    melon and ginger jam 26
    peach and passion fruit jam 22
    plum jam 20
    quick apricot jam 25
    rhubarb and strawberry jelly 35
    spicy blueberry jam 16
jelly
    cranberry jelly 30
    bell pepper and chile jelly 36
    pineapple and mint jelly 32
    tomato jelly 41
    wine jelly 38

kiwifruit
    orange and kiwi marmalade 55

lemon
    ginger citrus marmalade 46
    lemon and orange marmalade 49
    traditional lemon curd 58
lime
    ginger citrus marmalade 46

mango
    banana, mango, and date chutney 72
    sweet mango preserve 86
marmalade
    ginger citrus marmalade 46
    lemon and orange marmalade 49
    orange and kiwi marmalade 55
    orange and squash marmalade 52
    reduced sugar marmalade 50
    traditional chunky marmalade 44
melon
    melon and ginger jam 26
    melon rind pickle 82

orange
    apple and orange curd 64
    lemon and orange marmalade 49
    orange and kiwi marmalade 55

orange and squash marmalade 52
    reduced sugar marmalade 50
    traditional chunky marmalade 44
passion fruit
    apricot and passion fruit butter 66
    peach and passion fruit jam 22
peach
    peach and passion fruit jam 22
pear
    pear, cranberry, and celery root relish 78
pickles
    melon rind pickle 82
    mixed vegetable pickle 76
pineapple
    pineapple and mint jelly 32
plum
    plum butter 63
    plum jam 20
preserves
    berry preserve 91
    pepper pot preserve 94
    raspberry and apple preserve 92
    sweet beet preserve 88
    sweet mango preserve 86

raspberry
    berry preserve 91
    raspberry and apple preserve 92
relishes
    blueberry relish 81
    pear, cranberry, and celery root relish 78
rhubarb
    rhubarb and strawberry jelly 35

squash
    orange and squash marmalade 52
strawberry
    berry preserve 91
    classic strawberry jam 14
    rhubarb and strawberry jelly 35

tomato
    tomato chutney 75
    tomato jelly 41

wine
    wine jelly 38